# COLORING BOOK

THIS BOOK BELONGS TO:

# COLORING!

Sincere thanks for choosing our coloring book. That sounds great when knowing that you give it a lot of love. These funny activities like the perfect way to make you smile more and practice concentration.

Once you complete this book, you will get yourself very lovely spiritual gifts as souvenirs.

Thank you! Have fun and enjoy!

Visit our website to get more Free Digital Coloring Book!

HTTPS://ICOLORMYLIFE.COM/FREE-PRINT

## ICOLORMYLIFE.COM

# COLOR TEST PAGE

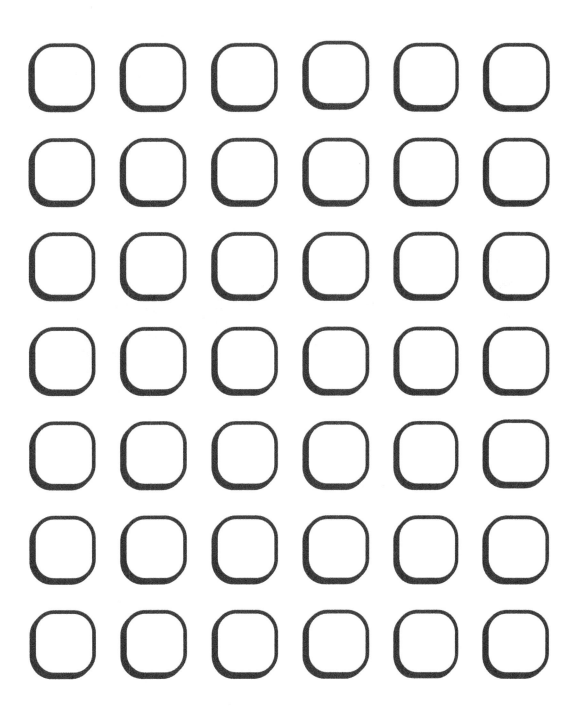

Coloring

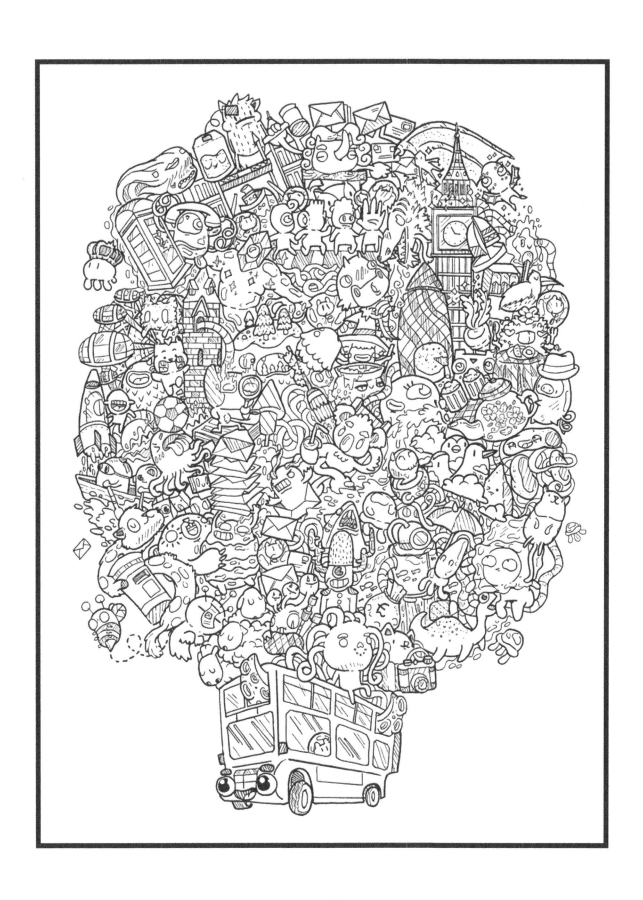

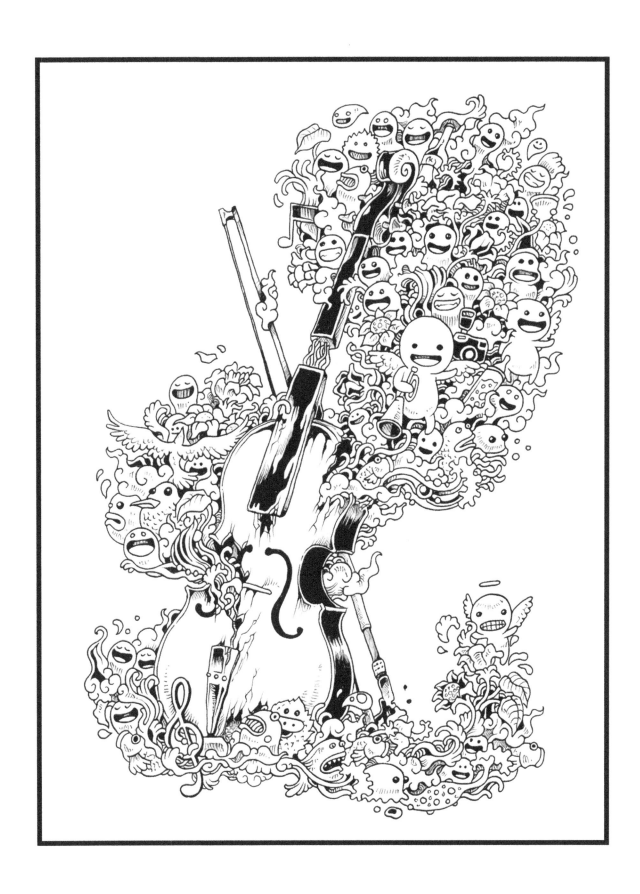

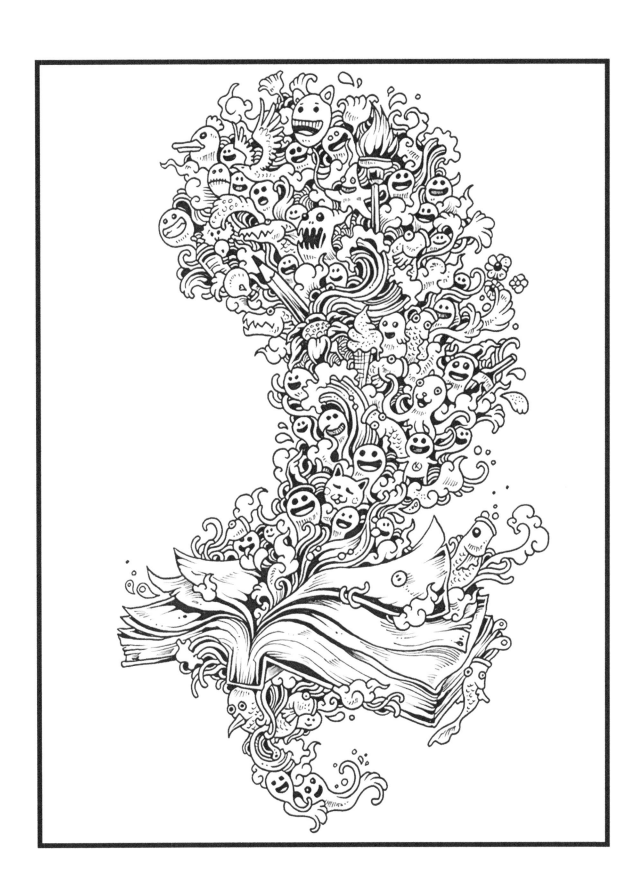

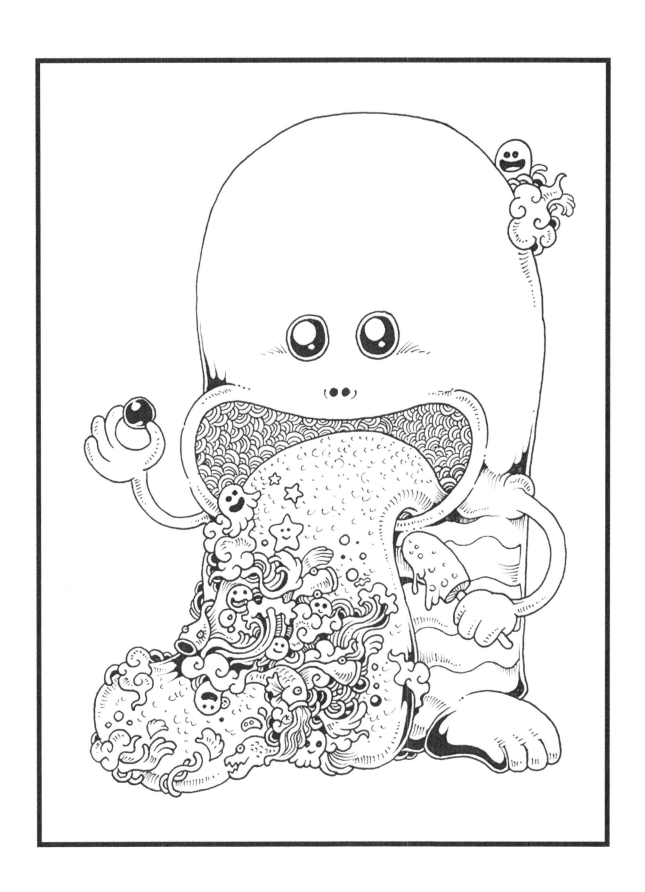

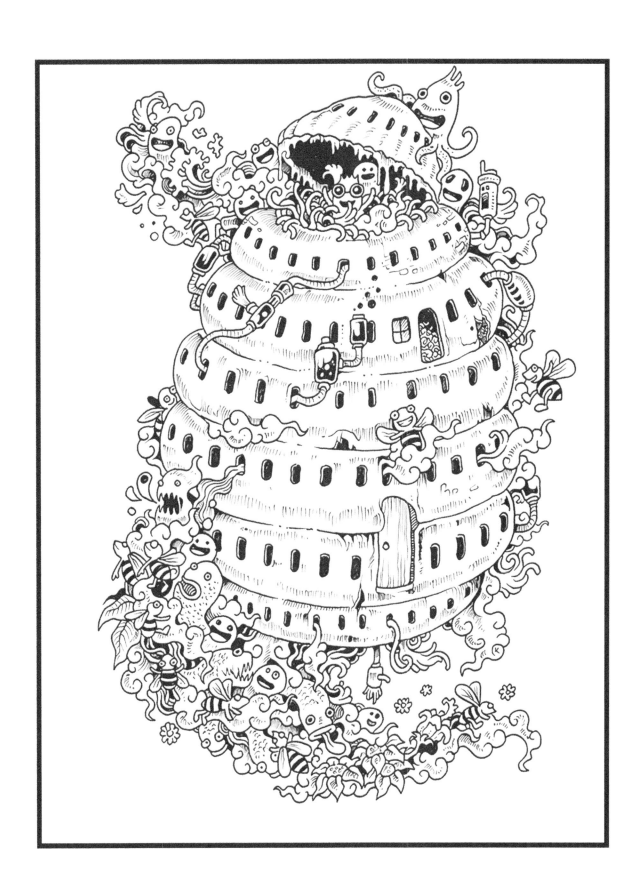

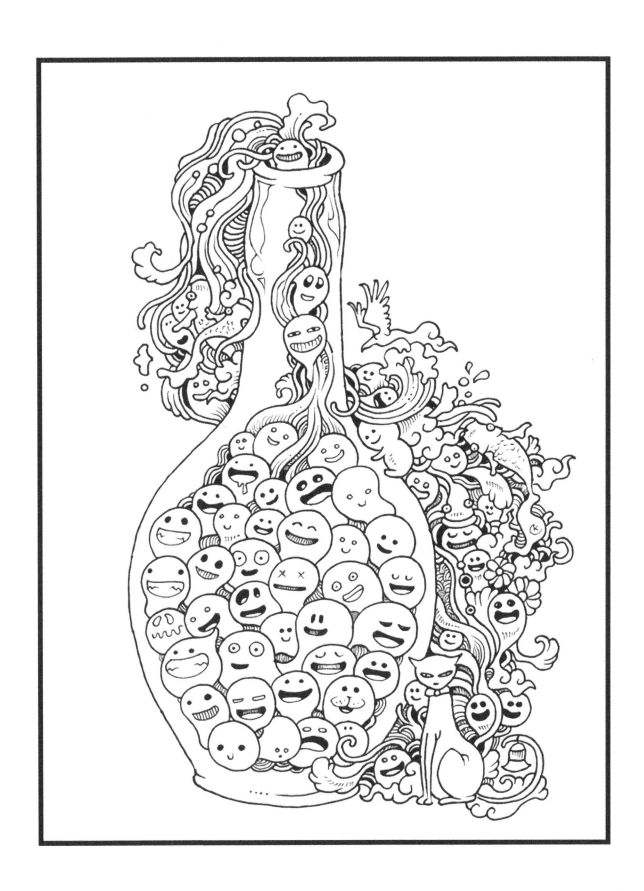

ICOLORMYLIFE

# THANK FOR TRUSTING
# AND CHOOSING OUR PRODUCT

VISIT OUR WEBSITE TO GET MORE FREE WONDERFUL PRODUCTS

HTTPS://ICOLORMYLIFE.COM/FREE-PRINT

**ICOLORMYLIFE.COM**

Made in the USA
Monee, IL
20 September 2024

66255374R00037